Seasons Change
by Beth Wells

Editorial Offices: Glenview, Illinois • Parsippany, New Jersey • New York, New York
Sales Offices: Needham, Massachusetts • Duluth, Georgia • Glenview, Illinois
Coppell, Texas • Sacramento, California • Mesa, Arizona

Photo locators denoted as follows: Top (T), Center (C), Bottom (B), Left (L), Right (R), Background (Bkgd)

Opener (CL) Digital Vision, Opener (BL) Brand X Pictures, Opener (BR) Brand X Pictures, Opener (CR) © Image Source/Superstock; 1 Image Ideas; 3 (TL) Digital Vision, 3 (BL) Brand X Pictures, 3 (BR) Brand X Pictures, 3 (TR) © Image Source/Superstock; 4 (C) Digital Vision, 4 (TL) Brand X Pictures, 4 (BL) Corel; 5 (C) © Image Source/Superstock, 5 (TR) Brand X Pictures, 5 (BR) © Frank Siteman/Index Stock Images; 6 (C) Brand X Pictures, 6 (TR) Brand X Pictures, 6 (CR) © Royalty-Free/Corbis, 6 (BR) Peter Pearson/ Getty Images; 7 (C) Brand X Pictures, 7 (T) Getty Images, 7 (BL) Corel; 8 Image Ideas

ISBN: 0-328-13193-8

Weather helps us learn about
the seasons.
Does it always feel the same outside?
Oh no, not when the seasons
change.

Good-bye, winter!
Spring is here.
It's warmer than before.

Good-bye, spring!
Summer is here.
It's the hottest time of all.

Good-bye, summer!
Fall is here.
It's cooler now.

Good-bye, fall!
Winter is here.
It's the coldest time of all.

How does it feel outside today?
The weather could be just right!
But it won't stay the same.
Seasons change!